走 近 故 宫

PHOTO–CRAWLING
the FORBIDDEN CITY

A Personal Retrospective of Li Shaobai

摄影／李少白

PUBLISHED BY CHINA ESPERANTO PRESS BEIJING   中国世界语出版社 北京

PREFACE

Li Shaobai

Auguste Rodin said to the effect that what is lacking is not beauty but the eye to discover it. The intention of the great virtuoso, I surmise, was to remind us not to neglect things which look plain and banal, for beauty is contained in them. I want to add, however, that while marvelling at the greatness of things that are out of the ordinary, we should guard against blind faith in beauty.

The sublimity of the Forbidden City is a self-evident fact. The pomp and pageantry of its architecture, and the grandeur of its scenes and sceneries, have enraptured so many visitors and inspired so many master artists. Whenever I set foot in this imperial palace of bygone days and contemplate the glory of the immense assemblage of classic architecture, my thoughts would turn to my predecessors' various portrayals of it, in rhetorics or pictorial renditions. While their depictions give me plenty of enjoyment, they fail to measure up to my vision of the Forbidden City, and thus leave me somewhat unsatisfied. As I gaze with longing eyes at the tall, vermillion walls, the question often pops into mind: What is it that brings me back, time and again, to this pile of old buildings? Having failed to find the answer in words, I have no choise but to go photo-crawling to find it. Peeping through my lenses at the cottony clouds hovering in the azure sky above the sober and rather melancholy walls, I often envision eunuchs staring at me with eyes at once sorrowful and hungry from dark corners. Whenever my camera catches the sight of tiny yellow flowers protruding from underneath a blue-stone wall, in my mind's eye I could see a palace maid dreaming in her sweet slumber. Whenever I set eye on a rusty lock that hangs heavy on a palace gate whose paint is peeling off, I sense I am dangerously close to the clue to some palace scandal that has been kept in the dark for so long.

From different viewpoints, in different lights, weathers and seasons, in panoramas or close-ups, I probe relentlessly in the Forbidden City for scenes that hold my heart intoxicated and my soul possessed. With the passing of time, my searches through the lenses have become so obstinate, and my daydreams so untrammelled, that I am gradually losing sight of the reality of the Forbidden City, and my vista has become as sharp as an awl piecing ever so slowly and tenaciously into the very fabric of Chinese history. There are neither clear explanations nor telltale revelations to what appears through my lenses. What is left is a mixture of impressions, hints, associations, poetry, and dreams.... Underneath the mystery of the Forbidden City lies the entangled mass of my thoughts.

自　序

李少白

罗丹有句名言："不是缺少美，而是缺少发现。"我想，大师的本意恐怕是提醒世人不要忽视平凡，美往往与平凡同在。可是我却觉得当人们仰视伟大的不平凡时，更需要警惕自己对美的盲目。

故宫的不平凡是不言而喻的。它的雄伟，它的壮丽，它的金碧辉煌，它的气象万千……不知被多少凡夫俗子称道过，又不知被多少才人巨匠描述过，然而当我每次走进这昔日的帝王之家，驻足凝神这宏伟的古建筑群时，脑海里不禁泛起前人对它有过的种种描绘，欣赏之后，不免总有些不满足的感叹。我心中的故宫似乎不尽是那样……面对着紫禁城，常常自问：是什么最使我心痴神迷，竟能一而再，再而三地徜徉在这高墙之下，深宫之内呢？我说不清楚，于是只有用我的相机的镜头去寻找答案了。当我的镜头对着阴森的宫墙一角那片蓝天里的一朵白云时，恐怕我无法躲开太监们那哀怨又充满渴望的目光，当我的镜头对着惨白的青石墙角下盛开着的一簇黄色的小花时，恐怕我拾到了一个至今还未醒转的宫女之梦，当我的镜头对着油漆剥落的宫门上那锈迹斑斑的沉重铁锁时，恐怕是无意中揭开了尘封多年的又一条宫帏密闻……我的镜头在紫禁城里不断地游移着，从俯瞰到仰视，从整体到局部，从不同的角落，不同的光线，不同的气候，不同的季节……寻找着最令我心醉神往的一切，久而久之，我发现我的镜头是这样固执，固执地睁眼做梦，竟渐渐地忘了故宫的真实；我的视角又是这样的狭窄，窄到有如锥子，竟慢慢刺进了那历史的沉淀……于是我惊叹：我的镜头中没有故宫的说明，没有故宫的解释，没有故宫的报道，剩下的或许只有感叹，只有暗示，只有联想，只有诗，只有梦……只有从紫禁城的神秘中泄露出来的我的错综复杂的心声。

LI SHAOBAI — A PROFILE

Li Shaobai, born in Chongqing in 1942, developed a liking for poetry while a child, thanks to the influence of his family. It seemed he was destined for the world of art, but by a twist of fate, he was enrolled in 1960 in the Beijing Institute of Physical Culture to learn how to play soccer. Before long he became a student in the Radio Department of the Beijing Institute of Posts and Telecommunications. During the tumultuous ten-year "cultural revolution", he was framed and spent the better part of a decade behind the bars. After he was exonerated he became a member of the computer department of the Beijing Medical Equipment Research Institute. It was then that he began to make a career out of photography. In 1984 he became a reporter and editor for the magazine *Bridge*, where he was later made director of the editorial department. In the intervening years he has built up a rich portfolio of photographs which enabled him to publish such books as *Selected Photographs by Li Shaobai*, *Mysterious Forbidden City* and *The Great Wall*. He has also held a personal retrospective show entitled "Mysterious Forbidden City". He is concurrently on the editorial boards of two journals, *China Photography* and *Photography and Cinematography*.

Among his numerous motifs the Forbidden City is his favorite. Why the former imperial palace, of all the wonderful things in this boundless universe? Just to quote himself, "Every time I visit the Forbidden City, I feel touched in a peculiar way." Whenever he clicks his camera, that peculiar feeling would well up in his heart and become fused with the subject, leaving a special, indelible image on the film. Perhaps because of this, he is able to emerge, from among a vast contingents of photographers who specialize on the Forbidden City, as a school of his own, a school marked by a distinctive personal style in composition and in the treatment of colour and light and shade. In one of his trenchant tableaus, shot with a wide-angle lens and from a worm's-eye view, the gravity and sheer height of two palace walls are so exaggerated as to literally squeeze the immense blue sky between them into a sword-like strip piecing the reigning darkness in a way that never fails to make the heart tremble; his contemplations of the former glory behind the tall walls are imbedded in the yellow-glazed eaves poised on juxtaposed red pillars. The modernistic style which characterizes his photography has stood him in good stead in reflecting his rich and profound inner world.

Shaobai explores the mystery of the Palace Museum with both lenses and heart. "Each time I ramble among the halls, terraces and pavilions under a different frame of mind, I see a different Palace Museum from a different angle and under a different light-and-shade effect, and the buildings which have been there for hundreds of years would echo in my heart and give me penetrating insight into new combinations and groupings. In the split second when the camera clicks, I bring home, on film, my own vision of the Palace Museum, which is a personification of myself."

This personal retrospective book, *Photo-Crawling the Forbidden City*, is yet another crop of masterpieces Li Shaobai has brought to readers in the wake of his *Mysterious Forbidden City*. As the titles suggest, both albums are about the same old theme, the Forbidden City, and we may well regard them as ingenious groupings of the author's richly variegated visions of the Forbidden City.

李少白简介

　　李少白,1942 年出生在重庆市,幼年受家庭的熏陶,喜欢诗赋。本该走进艺术天地的他,1960 年却到了北京体育学院主修足球,后又在北京邮电学院无线电系学习。"十年动乱"期间,他蒙冤蹲了近十年监狱。平反后,被安排到北京医疗器械研究所计算机室工作,并开始步入摄影界。1984 年,调入《桥》杂志社,历任记者、编辑、编辑室主任等职。在此期间,他的摄影事业也硕果累累:出版了个人摄影专集《李少白摄影作品选》、《神秘的紫禁城》和《伟大的长城》;并举办了《神秘的紫禁城》摄影艺术展。少白先生现任《中国摄影》、《摄影与摄像》杂志编委。在众多的摄影对象中,少白先生深深眷恋着故宫。大千世界,无奇不有,为什么选择故宫做摄影主题呢? 用他自己的话说,是因为"每一次去故宫,都会有一种特殊的感动。"正因为如此,在他举起相机按下快门时,那种特殊的感觉似乎融合到了镜头前的景物中,在胶片上产生了特殊效果。也正因为如此,在众多的故宫摄影专家中,少白先生的作品自成风格,在构图、色彩、影调等表现上均有独到之处。例如用广角镜头和低摄角度,夸张宫墙的高大深重,那两墙之间的一线蓝天,像一柄利刃,刺破黑暗,看了使人的心灵为之震颤。那整齐排列的大红柱间透出的一檐黄瓦,传达了作者对深院高墙内往昔幽思的感叹。凡此种种颇具现代派风格的表现方式,映照出了少白先生丰富深邃的内心世界。

　　少白先生用镜头,也用心去探索、去揭示故宫的奥秘。"我穿行在楼台亭阁中,在不同的角度、不同的光影效果、不同的心境下,我看到了不同的故宫,这时那些已矗立百年的建筑和我的心声相和,在我的感受中显现出新的排列、新的组合。当我按下快门的瞬间,我拍的已是我眼中的故宫,是反射着自己、人化着自己的故宫。"即将出版的《走近故宫》画册,就是少白先生继《神秘的紫禁城》之后,表现故宫这一特定摄影对象的又一力作,是少白化的故宫组合。

OUTER COURT

The Forbidden City was home to twenty-four emperors of the Ming (1368-1644) and Qing (1644-1911) dynasties. A street running by the Gate of Heavenly Purity divides the premises into the Outer Court and the Inner Court. Three halls — the Hall of Supreme Harmony, Hall of Complete Harmony and Hall of Preserving Harmony — constitute the centrepiece of the Outer Court. The Hall of Literary Glory and the Hall of Martial Valour that flank these three halls were main venues of the emperors' political activities. The buildings in the Outer Court are as a rule tall, imposing, and elaborately ornamented to symbolize the supremacy of the Forbidden City and the absolute authority of imperial power.

外　　朝

　　故宫是中国明(公元 1368 1644 年)、清(1644 1911 年)两代皇宫,曾有 24 位皇帝在此处理朝政和居住。它以乾清门前横街为界分为外朝、内廷两部分。外朝以太和、中和、保和三大殿为主体,左右衔连文华、武英两殿,是皇帝从事政务活动的主要场所。外朝建筑高大、宏阔、豪华,以表现皇家宫殿的至尊至贵以及皇权统治的绝对权威。

A PANORAMIC VIEW OF THE FORBIDDEN CITY A telephoto lens was used to pack the multitude of palaces into the limited space of this picture, whose visual appeal is enhanced by the light of the setting sun which serves to outline the buildings in distinct forms.

故宫远眺　使用长焦镜头,将宫殿压缩在一起,并利用斜阳勾勒出屋脊的轮廓,使古典建筑的魅力在形式美中体现出来。

A NOCTURNAL GLIMPSE OF THE CORNER TOWER This tableau, shot with a tele-photo lens and after a long exposure to night light, blends vermillion columns and windows into the warm colour of yellow. Due to the telephoto lens's image plane-compressing effect and the defusing nature of night light, the corner tower loses its three dimensional effect and acquires the breathtaking beauty of a unique plane pattern. In this way a poetic touch is added to photography's life-recording property.

角楼夜景 利用夜间灯光做光源,经过长时间曝光后,使红色的柱、窗都统一到温暖的黄色中。由于长焦的平面压缩性和夜间灯光的散射性,角楼的造型虽然失去了立体感,却形成一种很美的平面图案,摄影的纪实具有了画意。

SCARLET DUSK A classic scene tainted red in the twilight of the setting sun.

血色黄昏

THE MERIDIAN GATE BATHED IN SUN RAYS This photograph, taken by spotmetering the multi-hued clouds in the sky, captures a shaft of light which tosses a crazy-quilt pattern of cloud shadows onto the awesome form of the ancient structure.

午门飞霞　以天空彩云测光。变幻无常的天光云影,衬托出古老宫殿的威严。

EASTERN WILD GOOSE WING CHAMBER Vitality and tension are unmistakable in this photograph, taken with exposure on the sky and clouds reduced by a full stop to contrast, in a striking way, the dazzling sun with the overcast sky and the Forbidden City's dimly-lit wall.

东雁翅楼 比天空白云正常曝光减一档。光芒耀眼的太阳、浓云翻滚的天空与暗色的城楼产生强烈对比,使画面充满生命力和紧张感。

WEEPING WILLOWS Distinct contrast between substance and abstraction is achieved in this compact composition by giving full scope to the perspective effect of a lens of long focus length.

垂柳依依 利用长焦镜头压缩的透视效果,使画面紧凑,从而产生虚实对比。

WESTERN WILD GOOSE WING CHAMBER The use of a wide-angle lens helped to exaggerate the wall and make the flowers stand out in the foreground.

西雁翅楼 使用广角镜头,既夸张了城墙,又突出了前景的花朵。

RIGHT IMPERIAL GATE A 200-mm lens was used to capture on the same plane the golden-glazed tiles and the dark red palace gate at sunset. The shadow on the gate brings subtle changes to the symmetrical composition, adding a captivating liveliness to this solemn-looking picture.

阙右门 利用200毫米焦距,将夕阳下的金瓦与暗红色的宫门压缩在一个平面上,宫门上的阴影使对称的构图产生了微妙的变化,整幅面既庄严又富有生气。

INNER GOLDEN WATER RIVER Under the slanting morning sunlight, the white marble balustrades with its highlighted texture figure prominently as the main subject of this picture. Depth of field and nuance of detail are achieved by the use of a lens of short focus length.

内金水河 白玉石栏杆在晨光的斜照下成了质感突出的主题,短焦镜头的运用使画面既有深度,又有层次。

INNER GOLDEN WATER RIVER The blue sky and water surface serve to accentuate the vermilion walls and golden roofs of the Palace Museum at a moment when the sun was dipping below the horizon.

内金水河 深蓝的天空和水面,更能突出夕阳下宫殿的红墙黄瓦。

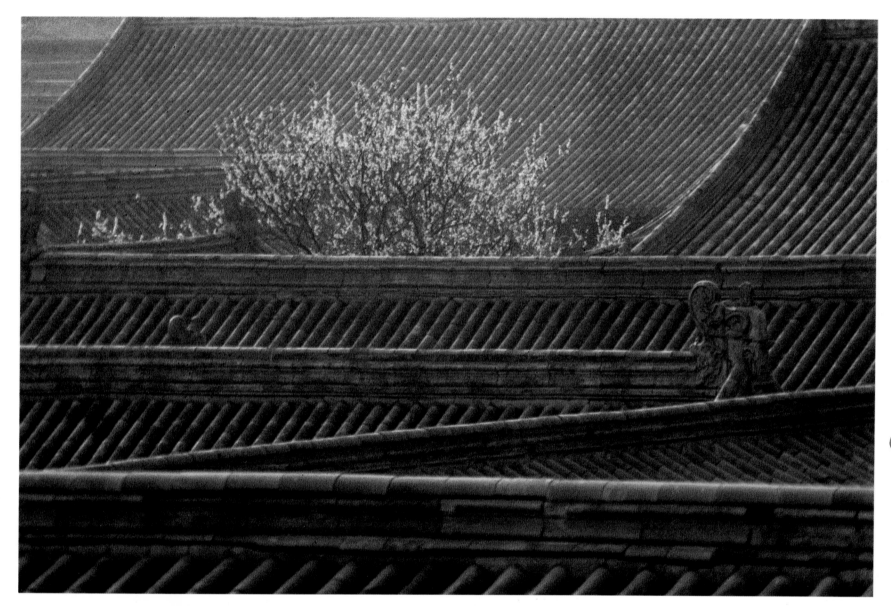

◀ **A SNOW-BOUND SCENE** A sense of rhythm is gained, and a touch of life are instilled into an otherwise harsh impression of the snow scene, in this picture which integrates the curves of the imperial river with the vertical lines of the posts in the marble balustrades. The liveliness of the picture is enhanced by setting the darkish water surface in contrast with the fallen snow.

白雪皑皑　御河的弧形与石栏的竖线形成的节奏感,避免了白茫茫冬景的呆板。幽暗的水面映衬出的落雪,更增加了勃勃生气。

IN THE DEPTH OF AN IMPERIAL COURTYARD Using a 400-mm telephoto lens at a commanding height, the author succeeded in photographing the rich pile of glazed-tile roofs in a wholesome picture, and touched it up with a cluster of apricot trees in full bloom in the heart of the Forbidden City. The presence of the blossoms serves to heighten the visual effect of the composition.

庭院深深　在一个较高的视点,用超长焦(400mm)将层层琉璃瓦屋顶压缩到一起,并将深宫中盛开的杏花拉进画面,造成强烈的视觉效果,成为"庭院深深深几许"的最好阐释。

TOWER OF ENHANCED RIGHTEOUSNESS The colour of light blue strikes a chilliness into the beholder, and the partial use of light serves to bring variation to the picture.

弘义阁　运用淡蓝色,使人产生冷感;使用局部光,使画面富于变化。

A LION BARKING AT THE SUN The bronze lion in the foreground is outlined in the twilight of the setting sun, while the Meridian Gate is silhouetted against the blue sky in a photograph whose remarkable simplicity gives much food for thought.

雄狮 利用夕阳勾勒出前景铜狮的雄姿,幽蓝的天空衬出午门的剪影,使画面极度简化,给观者留下无限的遐思。

A SILVERY WORLD The lines of white marble balustrades cocooned in a thick mantle of snow run gracefully across this picture. A balance in the composition is achieved by using a wide-angle lens to set distant palaces in striking contrast with foreground scenes.

粉琢玉砌 雪中白玉石栏杆贯穿着画面,远处宫殿在广角镜头突出前景的效果下,形成对比,并使画面平衡。

TOWER OF ENHANCED RIGHTEOUSNESS The silhouettes of the ancient building, old tree and crow render a poetic air to the Forbidden City at sunset.

弘义阁 古楼、老树、昏鸦,采用剪影的表现形式,使故宫暮色更具诗情画意。

THE FRONT COURTYARD OF THE HALL OF SUPREME HARMONY The dullness of the foggy light is broken, and necessary depth of field is yielded, in this picture by placing the white marble balustrades in the foreground.

太和殿广场　利用白玉石栏杆作前景,打破雾天光线的平淡,使画面产生了必要的纵深感。

THE FRONT COURTYARD OF THE HALL OF SUPREME HARMONY A wide-angle lens was used to highlight a ground strewn with ancient-looking bricks, thereby rendering a sense of history to the scene.

太和殿广场　用广角镜头突出前景狼藉满地的古砖,增强了历史沧桑感。

25

A SURREPTITIOUS PEEP AT THE FORBIDDEN CITY This dynamic-looking picture is made by setting off the darkish columns of a palace gallery against the well-illuminated palaces in the distance.

从贞度门看太和殿　画框前景暗色的廊柱与远处明亮的宫殿相互映衬、相互对比,形成一幅生动的图画。

TOWER OF MANIFESTING BENEVOLENCE AT SUNSET The setting sun serves to cheer up and "humanize" the forlorn and uninviting presence of the palaces.

体仁阁夕照　暖暖的夕阳,融和了清冷的宫殿,增加了浓浓的人情味。

A STUDY OF MINUTE DETAILS The Hall of Supreme Harmony integrates with white clouds, green grass, stone columns and ancient bricks to form an intricate pattern in this fascinating picture.

太和殿 白云、绿草、石柱、古砖,形成了细节性的结合,使画面更显生动。

HALL OF SUPREME HARMONY The darkish stone columns serve to reiterate the architectural pomp and decorative pageantry of the Hall of Supreme Harmony.

太和殿　深色的石柱,突出了太和殿的金碧辉煌。

THREE-TIERED TERRACE Light and dark objects in the foreground are compressed into this study of contrast between light and shadow.

丹陛 利用长焦镜,将明暗前景压缩在一起,产生强烈的对比。

PERMUTATIONS AND COMBINATIONS Surveying the scene ever so painstakingly with a telephoto lens, the author discovers exactly what he wants: the repeated permutations and combinations of horizontal, vertical and oblique lines, which pumped a sense of rhythm into the works of classical Chinese architecture.

排列组合 用长焦镜细心寻找到一个恰当的画面:横线、竖线、斜线交错排列,重复出现,表现古典建筑的节奏感。

THREE-TIERED TERRACE Looking down at the Forbidden City through his camera from a unique angle, the artist discerns a sense of rhythm in this group of ancient buildings, and the visual effect of this picture is enhanced by the felicitous use of light and shadow.

丹陛 镜头俯视,从另一个视角体察古典建筑的节奏感,其中光影的运用更增强了这种视觉效果。

THE SCULPTURE OF A HORNLESS DRAGON HEAD With the aid of a telephoto lens, this photograph positions the marble balustrades in the intermediary range and the distant palaces in the background, with attention focused on the hornless dragon head in the foreground. Only with a focus of attention can a photograph acquire a well-defined meaning.

螭首 长焦镜头将前景的螭首、中景的石栏和远景的宫殿压缩在一起，并将螭首放置在画面的趣味中心。布局紧凑并突出趣味中心,才能使一张照片有明确的含义。

CENTRAL-LEFT GATE The eye is delighted by the balustrades of white marble, pulled into focus from the distance with a telephoto lens to form an intriguing combination with tall red-lacquered gallery columns.

中左门 利用长焦镜头,将远处的白玉石栏杆拉近,与高大的红色廊柱组成饶有趣味的画面。

A SCENE OF ENCHANTING BEAUTY The use of a wide-angle lens yielded this tableau ▶ which encapsulates the marble balustrades and halls in the distance while focusing attention to the loftiness of the palace gate. The sober and melancholy atmosphere of the snow-covered Forbidden City is shown with a measured sense of propriety by contrasting the snowy courtyard with the gloomy-looking palace gate.

别有洞天 广角镜头不仅将远处的石栏、宫殿尽收画面,而且将宫门表现得格外高大,洁白的庭院、幽暗的宫门对比强烈,雪后故宫的森严和冷寂得到了恰当表现。

36

HALL OF COMPLETE HARMONY AND HALL OF PRESERVING HARMONY The cottony clouds scudding across the sky, and the scar-pockmarked bricks, seem to bespeak of the merciless passage of time and the complexity of this mundane world.

中和殿和保和殿 飞扬流动的白云、斑痕累累的青砖悄悄告诉人们:岁月无情,世事沧桑。

REAR-RIGHT GATE

后右门

HALL OF GATHERING "WAY" The trees, throwing their shadows into the foreground, serve to make up for the desolation and emptiness of the bridge surface.

凝道殿 利用树影充当前景,弥补了桥面的空荡。

BROKEN-RAINBOW BRIDGE Under the shiny sun willow tree branches sway gently in the wind, while clusters of wild flowers gleam in dark foreground shadows. The advent of spring finds apt expression in this picture in which action echoes non-action in a congenial way.

断虹桥 明亮的阳光下,柳枝迎风飞舞;而在前景的暗影中,几簇野花静静地开放。盎然的春意就在这一动一静的呼应中得到了充分体现。

43

JIHUA GATE A shaft of light struggles dimly through the obscurity of a palace door in this thought-provoking photograph.

基化门 幽暗的宫门,透出些许光线,令人浮想联翩。

SOARING INTO THE SKY Seen through a 18-mm lens, this ancient edifice soars into the vault of heaven in a heroic fashion.

与天争雄 古老的宫殿通过18mm镜头显示出与蓝天争雄的气概。

BEHIND A ROYAL STUDY. Willow branches, whirling gracefully against a blue sky, are set against the shadows of swaying trees on a vermillion wall in this composition, looking rich and orderly thanks to provident contrasts between light and shade, between cool and warm colour tones, and between substance and abstraction.

缮书房后 蓝天映衬着的婀娜的柳枝与红墙上婆娑的树影形成光的明暗对比、色的冷暖对比、物的虚实对比，使画面既丰富又有秩序。

PALACE GATE The meticulous portrayal of the details, coupled with the effect of the slanting light, seems to render some vitality to this partial study of a palace gate.

宫门 局部的描写,细节的刻画,斜光的效果,使剥落的宫门"无声胜有声"。

PALACE GATE A striking contrast between the three primary colours of red, yellow and blue, supplemented with changes in light and shade, enables the artist to depict the beauty of colour of this ancient building in a way so impeccable as to bar any suggestion of monotony.

宫门 通过红、黄、兰三原色的强烈对比,辅以光影变化,将表现中国古典建筑色彩美的画面处理得既有规律又不单调。

INNER COURT

The Inner Court, situated north of the three major halls, is divided into three sections. The central section consists of the Hall of Heavenly Purity, Hall of Union and Peace, and Hall of Earthly Tranquility, with the Imperial Garden in the rear. The eastern section, i.e., the Six Eastern Palaces, sprawls symmetrically with the western section, i. e., the Six Western Palaces, across the Axial Line. The Hall for the Worship of Ancestors, the Hall of Abstinence and the Princes' Studies (otherwise known as Three Southern Abodes) are found south of the Six Eastern Palaces, while the Hall of Mental Cultivation stands south of the Six Western Palaces. The Inner Court is flanked by the building complex of the Palace of Tranquil Longevity to the east and the Hall for the Consolation of Mothers and the Hall of Peaceful Old Age to the west. The Inner Court, known to the public as "Three Palaces and Six Courtyards", was where the emperor and his royal family resided and spent their time of leisure. It was where the retinue of emperor's kept ladies whiled away their hours; it is the place to be for those curious about life behind the walls of the Forbidden City.

内　　廷

三大殿以北为内廷,内廷又分中、东、西三路。中为乾清宫、交泰殿、坤宁宫,其后是御花园;中路两侧为东、西六宫。东六宫向南是奉先殿、斋宫、南三所,西六宫往南为养心殿。内廷外围东有宁寿全宫,西有慈宁、寿安诸宫。内廷即俗称的"三宫六院",是皇帝及其家属居寝和憩息之所。这里时时处处晃动着帝后妃嫔们的影子,是探访禁宫生活的最佳去处。

BRONZE CALDRONS Using a telephoto lens, the photographer cuts the "fat" from the "lean" to perceive a fully composed picture of an array of bronze caldrons.

铜缸 长焦镜头将排列成队的铜缸略加压缩,不仅使画面紧凑,而且摈除了多余景物,突出了主题。斜光的照射使铜缸富于立体感,增强了画面美。

IMPERIAL GARDEN Distinction of the pavilion is gained by positioning it where the perspective lines converge. The big tree to the right brings balance to the composition.

御花园　将楼阁置于透视线会聚处,显得格外醒目;右侧的大树起着平衡画面的作用。

BRONZE LION In a dramatic play of the snow, this picture turns a bronze lion into something of a Peking Opera clown.

铜狮　雪,能给事物带来戏剧般的变化,雪后的铜狮简直成了京剧舞台上的喜剧角色。

◀ AGE VS. YOUTH: IMPERIAL GARDEN The effects of light and shade are employed with great felicity to set a time-worn bronze caldron in stark contrast with youthful-looking flowers.

御花园 暗旧的铜缸与明艳的花朵利用光影效果更能显出古拙和青春的强烈对比。

LOTUS POND From a vertical angle this close-up shows a lotus leaf beautified by ripples of rain on it. The colour of the picture is enriched, and the leaf's smooth and moist texture is depicted in vivid detail, by using well-diffused light, which eliminated glaring contrast and avoided the detraction of the shadows.

睡莲浮碧 镜角俯视能更好地表现荷叶、荷花的形状和水面上雨点的涟漪。柔和的散射光避免了强烈反差,也消除了阴影干扰,使荷叶质感细腻润泽,色彩更加饱和。

PAVILION OF A THOUSAND AUTUMNS Shooting with the aid of a telephoto lens, the author created an amazing abstraction of the scene by packing the foreground and background into the same image plane. The slanting light conjures up sharp and vigorous lines to the entire composition.

千秋亭　长焦镜头将前景、中景、后景几乎都压缩在一个视平面上，产生了抽象化的图案美。斜射光使画面线条显得更清晰有力。

WONDERLAND Golden rooftops, a statuesque rock, the trunk of a gingko tree, as well as their shadows were compressed by a telephoto lens onto a vermillion wall in the background, thereby yielding a picture which is evocative of some fairy tale.

童话世界　金色瓦顶、太湖山石、银杏树干再加上它们的光影都被长焦镜头压缩在背景红墙上，交织成一个奇特而又颇具童话色彩的画面。

GATE OF COMPLAISANT CHASTITY The liberal use of dim colour tone sets the stage for a stray of morning sunlight to penetrate the corner of a terrace and a palace gate in a composition so simplified as to give wings to imagination.

顺贞门 大面积的暗色调,是为了突出朝阳沐浴的一角楼台和从宫门里射出的一束光线。简洁的画面是为了强调描写重点,更好地激发读者想象力,释放自己的潜在感受。

HALL OF ABSTINENCE Against a backdrop formed by the ▶ Hall of Abstinence and the vermillion colour of the gate, screen wall and windows, snow flakes swirl about in what looks like a raging snowstorm.

斋宫 红门、红影壁、红窗作背景,映衬出飞舞的雪花,营造出宫庭大雪纷飞的气氛。

LEFT JINGUANG GATE The silhouettes quivering in a pool of rain serve to bring balance and aesthetic appeal to this picture.

近光左门 雨中的倒影，不仅平衡了画面，亦增加了情趣。

HALL OF SINCERITY AND SOLEMNITY Golden-glazed tiles and white snow glisten in the lateral-front light while a ray of the sun penetrates in between the dark-red columns of a gallery. The charm and mystery of the palace shine forth in this unique picture taken right after a snowstorm.

诚肃殿　在顺侧光下,金瓦闪烁,白雪晶莹,暗红的廊柱间透出一线光亮。雪后宫殿的妩媚和神秘交织在一起,营造出别具情趣的意境。

A WORLD UP THE SLEEVES The limited tolerance of reversal film robbed the shadows in this picture of their depth, but it helps accentuate the spring scene of the imperial palace on a sunny day.

深宫 反转片有限的宽容度,使阴影丧失了层次,却因此突出了我们想表现的丽日下的宫庭春景。

HALL OF QUINTESSENCE When photographing the cramped space of a tiny courtyard, only by using a wide-angle lens can the perspective be expanded and the picture look rich and meaningful.

钟粹宫 在狭小的庭院内，只有广角镜头才能扩大视角，使画面丰富。

HALL OF QUINTESSENCE "Framing" the principal object by means of doors and windows adds a sense of space to the picture and heightens the decorative effect on it.

钟粹宫 利用门窗作"画框"，既增强了空间感又起到了装饰作用。

A SCENE OF DESOLATION The flatness of ambient light comes in handy when depicting the gloom and desolation of autumn on its last legs.

瑟瑟 散射光的平淡正适合表现残秋的抑郁和凄凉。

SPRING DREAM IN THE DEPTH OF THE IMPERIAL PALACE With the image plane ▶ compressed by the use of a telephoto lens, an intricate relationship is fostered between pear flowers and a palace wall, making one wonder whether this picture is the dream of a palace maid or the wish of a prince on a spring day.

深宫春梦 长焦镜带来的平面压缩性,使梨花和宫墙是这样密不可分,因此极易产生遐想:是宫女未醒的春梦,还是王子萌动的希望……

67

HALL OF RECEIVING CELESTIAL FAVOUR Strong contrasts between light and darkness, red and yellow, light and shade, and between vertical and slanting lines, serve to dilute the tranquility of the scene at the end of a snowstorm in this abstract photograph.

承乾宫 明与暗、红与黄、光与影、直线与斜线的强烈对比,冲淡了雪后的宁静,产生了一种抽象的效果。

HALL OF JUSTICE

景阳宫

GALLERY COLUMNS The juxtaposed vertical lines of tall columns gleam with their outlines effectively highlighted in lateral backlight.

廊柱 高大廊柱重复的垂直线条是这幅照片的主题。在侧逆光的照射下,轮廓的阴影得到了强调。

SPRING RAIN IN THE IMPERIAL PALACE The author amused himself with this meticulous study of the wet brick-paved foreground, reflecting the drizzle which moistens the multitude of things in silence. The half-hidden green tree in the focus of attention adds a surprising touch of colour to the rain-drenched courtyard.

深宫春雨 通过对前景湿漉砖地的精心刻画,强调了润物无声的扉扉细雨;而出现在画面趣味中心的半掩绿树,给庭院雨景增添了令人意外的色彩效果。

A SKYWARD VIEW Few visitors care to lie down on the ground of the Forbidden City and take a look at the sky. This changed perspective enables the author to make an ordinary scene look extraordinary.

举头望天 走进故宫的人,很少躺在地上仰望,由于改变了视角,平常的景色变得不平常了。

SIX WESTERN PALACES FROM A SOUTHERN PERSPECTIVE The pomp and pageantry of the former imperial palace are reflected in this rendition of rows of golden-glazed tile roofs gleaming in the midst of green foliages.

南望西六宫　几丛绿树掩映着一片金黄色的瓦顶,通过镜头表现了故宫的金碧辉煌。

A PATHWAY IN THE SIX WESTERN PALACES In this shifting scene of light and shade, the narrow path looks even narrower to conjure up an oppressive atmosphere.

西六宫甬道 借助光影变化,使狭窄的甬道愈显狭窄,增强了压抑感。

ANCIENT CALDRONS IN THE FORBIDDEN CITY

深宫古缸

A BRONZE DRAGON ATOP THE HALL OF PRESERVING EL-EGANCE Rainy scenes can be indirectly portrayed through dampened subjects, as is the case with this picture.

储秀宫铜龙 雨景有时可以通过被打湿的物体来间接表现。

◀ **A BRONZE DRAGON LYING IN THE SNOW** The regular triangular composition renders a touch of composure and solemnity to the bronze dragon, lying in the snow against a dark background in this impressive picture.

铜龙卧雪 暗色的背景,正三角形的构图,使雪中铜龙显得沉稳和威严,给人留下深刻的印象。

77

BRONZE LION The use of a telephoto lens enabled the author to rid the picture of superfluous objects and draw attention to the bronze lion itself. The vermillion palace gate, blurred through the wide aperture of the lens, serves to indicate the environment and set the subject in relief.

铜狮 长焦距摈除了画面上多余的物体,使视线集中到铜狮身上,大光圈虚化的红色宫门既交代了周围环境,又有利于衬托主体。

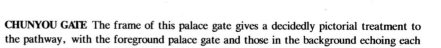

CHUNYOU GATE The frame of this palace gate gives a decidedly pictorial treatment to the pathway, with the foreground palace gate and those in the background echoing each other to yield depth of field and a sense of rhythm.

纯祐门　透过宫门拍摄甬道,可突出"画框"特色,使前后宫门遥相呼应,既增加了纵深感又富于节奏感。

IMPERIAL GARDEN A dark colour tone dominates this picture to emphasize a scene of howling wind and weeping rain.

乾隆花园 大面积运用暗色调，营造出凄风苦雨的气氛。

HALL OF TRANQUIL LONGEVITY The fallen flowers in the foreground are stressed with a wide-angle lens to play up the melancholy atmosphere that reigns over the ancient palace.

宁寿宫 广角镜强调了近景的落花,渲染了古老宫殿的淡淡哀愁。

83

JOCKEYING FOR POSITION An unusual beauty of form was achieved through the use of a 400-mm telephoto lens, which compressed the entire building complex of the Six Western Palaces onto a single image plane.

勾心斗角 利用400mm超长焦将西六宫的前后殿压缩在一个平面上,产生了不寻常的形式美。

A THEATRE IN THE IMPERIAL PALACE

扮戏楼

SPRING UNTRAMMELLED The darkness of a wall occupying two thirds of this photograph is broken by the blue sky in the shape of an inverted triangle. The sun ray and the spray of blooming apricot flowers combine to form a visual contract against the dark wall to relive the mood depicted in this line: "A spray of red apricot flowers breaks free and protrudes from atop a tall wall."

春色关不住 虽然占画面三分之二的墙体是如此黑暗,但是倒三角形的蓝天却打破了这黑色的沉重,一束阳光在高墙上所形成的光域和盛开的杏花连在一起,既与暗色墙体形成了视觉反差,也体现了"一枝红杏出墙来"的意境。

◀ **WONDERLAND** Making use of the role of the mist in obliterating superfluous details and adding to the depth of space, the author made the Forbidden City look like a veritable wonderland in heaven.

人间仙境 雾可以消除多余的细节, 亦可以增加空间纵深感。利用雾的这种特性, 可以将帝王之家表现成天上仙阙。

CORNER TOWER ATOP THE WALL OF THE FORBIDDEN CITY The monotony and gloom of this night scene is avoided with the clever use of lighting.

角楼 夜景的拍摄如果恰当利用了灯光, 就可打破黑色的单调与沉闷。

◀ **SUPERNATURAL CREATION** The dark wall and white snow combine to create a superb work of abstract photography.

巧夺天工 深色的城墙和洁白的落雪构成了一幅巧夺天工的抽象画。

AN IMPOSING IMAGE Under noontime sunlight which plunges head-on from the sky, the flying eaves of a corner pavilion throws its thick shadows upon the scene, and the resultant sharp contrasts between yellow and blue and between yellow and black serve to reiterate the beauty of colour and form of this ancient building.

巍巍 正午的顶射光造成了角楼飞檐下浓重的阴影,形成了黄与蓝、黄与黑的强烈对比,更能突出古建筑的色彩美和形式美。

A GLIMPSE OF THE FORBIDDEN CITY This picture of row upon row of roofs covered with yellow-glazed tiles, created with the aid of a telephoto lens, provides penetrating insight into the grand and sublime prospects of an ocean of palaces.

望故宫 通过长焦镜头截取故宫一角,这一片鳞次栉比、错落有致的瓦顶可以使我们想象到宫殿之海的壮观和美丽。

FORBIDDEN CITY SEEN FROM THE PROSPECT HILL Peeping through a telephoto lens right after a snowfall, the author perceived this all-encapsulating view of the Palace Museum from the top of the Prospect Hill.

从景山望故宫　俯视的镜角最能展现事物的全貌。登上景山最高处,用长焦镜头俯视,雪后故宫尽收眼底。

BRONZE LION UNDER A SNOW MANTLE The maximum depth of a lens of short focus length has ensured maximum sharpness in the image of objects in front of and behind the focused distance in this picture.

雪狮子　短焦镜头的大景深特性保证了画面前、中、后三景的清晰度。

A GLANCE AT THE FORBIDDEN CITY The clusters of modern buildings which surround the Forbidden City having been obliterated in dense fog, the mass of palaces and pavilions in this picture evinces an air of nostalgia and classic sanctity.

望故宫 浓雾隐去了现代化的城市建筑,当眼前只剩下巍峨的宫殿和高耸的楼台,心头便升起了思古之幽情。

责任编辑　　施永南
翻　译　凌　原
装帧设计　　蔡　荣
Editor in Charge: Shi Yongnan
Translated by Ling Yuan
Designed by Cai Rong

图书在版编目(CIP)数据

走近故宫/李少白摄.一
北京:中国世界语出版社,1997.9
ISBN 7 - 5052 - 0326 - 6
I.走... II.李... III.故宫－摄影集 IV.K928·74－64
中国版本图书馆 CIP 数据核字(97)第 15845 号

中国世界语出版社出版
(北京阜成门外百万庄路 24 号)
北京博诚印刷厂印刷
新华书店经销
开本 245×260mm　1/12　8 印张　10 千字　81 彩图
1997 年第一版第一次印刷
ISBN 7 - 5052 - 0326 - 6/J.39
定价:88.00 元

First edition 1997
ISBN 7 - 5052 - 0326 - 6
Published by China Esperanto Press, Beijing
24 Baiwanzhuang Road, Beijing,
China, 100037
08800

Printed in the People's Republic of China